Protest and Isolation

Edward L. Canavan

Copyright© 2020 Edward L. Canavan
ISBN: 978-93-90202-46-1

First Edition: 2020
Rs. 200/-

Cyberwit.net
HIG 45 Kaushambi Kunj, Kalindipuram
Allahabad - 211011 (U.P.) India
http://www.cyberwit.net
Tel: +(91) 9415091004 +(91) (532) 2552257
E-mail: info@cyberwit.net

Printed at Repro India Limited.

Contents

Foreword

The poems contained herein are arranged chronologically from March 19 to July 10, 2020, encompassing the start of the Los Angeles "Safer at Home" measure due to the rampant spread of COVID-19, the unrest and protests triggered by the death of George Floyd on May 26, and the violent, undisciplined actions of various police departments; as well as the severe political incompetence which continues as of this writing.

Edward L. Canavan

July 15, 2020

[crux of the matter]

obfuscation the rule

the truth
must be sought
and deciphered

pay no mind
to the fool at the podium

we are on our own

so find your light

and shine.

[closer to somewhere]

strangeness surrounds

time spans elastic
while space constricts

wireless the arteries of connection
society from a distance

face to face from screen to screen

an untouchable utopia
becomes our saving grace.

[shades of day]

all the whiles
slowed to a crawl

examining the walls
with a fine-toothed neurosis

a few voices
here and there

windows cracked for
a semblance of fresh air

heart and mind widened

wingspan stretched
to accommodate these spacious new hours
waiting to be filled.

[hold the line]

fire is the way
to walk thru

to use its burn
and warmth
to advantage

to not turn away
in its presence…

we are meant not to fight it…
but to harness it

to embrace it
to make it ours

to solder our armor and forge our path
and to leave a blazing trail as a beacon
for those still searching for light.

[solitude and redemption]

well tread roads
smolder in the rearview

sharply turned presence
now finely tuned

white calm walls
of empty rooms
to stand and stare

warm jets
of haunting gray slowness
surround

this history unmade
within the unknown

as a barely audible hymn of hope
hums beneath the static.

[as chills strum my spine]

a glass metamorphosis
sparsely occupies this gray morning

upon awakening
this chasm begged a crossing

building
toward a quiet mad rush
thru the vortex of my solitude.

[1x1]

cleanse and repeat
today it rains

a simple reminder
that nature can still be kind

a needed lesson
in the current climate

i gather my gloves and mask
and take to the empty streets

to walk this earth
toward a horizon
that continues to change by the minute

like it always has.

[infinite paradox]

as uncharted
as it may seem to be
we know things
in the darkness

deep and dazzling
corners illuminated
only by the absence of light

where our shadows congregate
in mutual solace

sharing secrets
from the other side
of visibility

which hold
all the keys we need
to continue living
in the light.

[regaining consciousness]

pulled under
by tendency
and influence

muddled and unmiddled

hawks and crows
circling the sun

too long the soul untouched
too far the distance to the heart

even if only for an instant
the feeling overwhelms

triggering response
to calmly return

to the spaces
in between thoughts

where peace
and solace
reside.

[far from gone]

here amidst the unnamed days
the hours of little use

scraps of madness and poetry
holding it all together

voices of loved ones
and words from the wise

sorting thru lies, propaganda,
bullshit, and hearsay

looking back,
looking ahead

but history shows us only
what cannot be changed

and the future can
tell us nothing

it is only the present
that can give us the
hope we seek.

[retrograde]

primitive transmissions
orbiting thru oblivion

from the silver beginnings
of stars and silence broken

to endless battle
in corridors of power
over useless talismans

to further obscure the lines
between freedom and exile.

[rest in being]

breathe easy

the hours are on fire
and the days are getting sicker

better to be alone
than holding anyone's hand

see the sun from where you are
and let your heart smile

the government is lying
and the world is on edge

best to laugh out loud
and avoid the black holes of
policy and propaganda put forth

catch the moon with your phone
and share it with the bright circles with whom
you have virtually surrounded yourself

as it becomes harder and harder to deny,
but sadly not as hard to believe, that far
too many people will wait to be shamed
into doing what is right

just concentrate
on being the good
that is needed now

and promise yourself
to keep doing the same
once this is all over.

[centerpiece of hollow]

circles within
holding the walls at bay

distance creeps closer

unburdened by wisdom
bent to deter and jeopardize

to swarm and ignore

generations of swine and smugness
full of groundless theory opposed
to proven truth

no regard
no accountability

obliviously holding court
on the wrong side of history

as it collapses
in on itself.

[in the valley of shadows]

cracked bells shudder
in the dense fog of birdcall

dreams leap from the trees
sparked by fear

falling freeways into the abysmal garden
of the empty river i walk beside

these ghost-town mornings
somehow soothe the soul

no footsteps
no bustle

with everything to do
but nowhere to go.

[solitary refinement]

clamor removed
time drifts into the ether
its frame dissolved

a serpent of ash
amidst the ruins
ceaselessly uncoils

as vestiges of unbecoming
occupy the space
between these walls.

[what is here]

no shore

an unfamiliar vastness
hitherto unseen

distraction too easy an answer
better to sit with this new unknown

let it in
find out where it leads the heart
and what it makes us feel

occupy its space
and examine it
from within

from different angles,
in different light

open up to hear
what it might be telling us
about ourselves

and to contemplate
what it reveals

explore the myriad vantages
before just dismissing its energy as

something to be passively and
begrudgingly waited out

for everything that happens
becomes part of the whole

and the more of it we ignore
the less of the big picture we
are able to see.

[new wilderness]

honing presence from
behind closed doors

treading lightly thru
the landscape of the psyche

wary of triggers and traps

the snares of fear and the
pitfalls of distractional avoidance

the futile strategies of
lasting comfort and security

resolved to find the strength
and cultivate the instinct

to remain both aware
and undeterred

amidst this perfect storm
of sickness and uncertainty.

[psychologically overcast]

slow time crawls
along fine lines

careful not to ignore discomfort
nor indulge its complaints

but to hold it
in the open spaces
now afforded

provisions met for the most part
turning focus to wider eyes
for brighter vision

tuning concentration
to deeper waves

outward from the heart

to those clearing a path
thru this dense new wilderness
of human nature

and to those being strangled
by its deadly vines.

[enemy mind]

submission relents
as the day truly breaks

mist and fog boiled away
the springtime of sickness persists

blinds rattle like death
in the hot wind

safely sheltered
from the outside

but completely vulnerable
to the threats from within.

[lambs & lions]

in a corner of sun
shadows cross the mind's eye

better for the time away
solitary progress maintained

deep dives and
wanderings of the psyche

documenting the days
somewhat safely from the shelter of home

while outside
the flowers are still flowers

the birds still sing
spring is still spring

oblivious to humanity's dark current
of quarantine and lockdown

still shining
and marching on
quite contently
without us.

[trust the gold]

tremors unearthed
beneath and beyond the waves

a glimmer thru the cracks
of numberless facades

present from inception
suddenly glimpsed
in a flash of clarity

a reminder
that within us all
there lay a gleaming and solid foundation
here from the very start.

[gone from going]

birdsong at sunset
the low light of dusk
fitting the mood

letting the night sink in
draping these bones
in the blue darkness
of solitude

as another day
begins its drift
toward the gallows
of memory.

[facing the void]

low in the light of the day
obsessing over things gotten away

subtle signs
from the dark places of the heart
heavy with both the eternal and the absurd

reaching for lost reflections
in the cracked mirror of passing time

toward the further unfolding
of our being.

[same as never]

caught in the clang
of a cracked bell

painful echoes
of nothing familiar

the hours stretch
like some lost road
toward a dim and
fogged horizon

no use to dwell or fret
over wheels already set in motion

destinations as yet undetermined

all the more reason
to seize these strange days

and to recalibrate the coordinates
toward our brightest inner horizons

to at least assure
that if we trip or stumble

we can still fall
in the right direction.

[out of season]

there are many places here
converging points of entry
forming a new impetus contingent
upon a forward trajectory

this pause allows the groundwork
to set a different stage

to mine the absence
and gather momentum
from the stillness

to discard what has served its purpose
and to proceed with the idea that the former normal
is far below that to which we should aspire.

[beyond belief]

gone from the other side
secrets arrive in places of unknowing

to urge us forward
to step ahead into who we are now to be

that who we always are and have been

where the wound
we thought prevented us
from moving forward

is in fact
what opens up our soul
to the world;

an invitation
we can no longer refuse.

[rest]

hammer lifting
as dusk sets the evening in motion
and another day winds down

i surrender the words
to the coming hours' darkness
stretch my length across the couch
and let the mind soak in the blue light
of satellite transmissions

leaving midnight
to write the last lines
and turn the page.
***

[time enough]

ancient equations
rent the silent air

forwardness hobbled
by hindsight's blind spots

rogue eras stranded
outside the clock

compassion stillborn

as the mindless
emerge with a vengeance
from the unbearable inconvenience
of being asked to adhere to common sense,
decency, and courtesy

over pompousness and privilege.

[the burning down]

caught in breaking storms
of terrible wonder

cities alight
with retribution
and demand

nothing waits
for better times

this is not a new revolution

the civil war never ended
there is no equality

the rights promised
and never granted
will now be taken

the darkness
is now in the light

may it lead the way
to a level ground

and if the current ground
need be torched
in the process

so be it.

[out of time]

known enemies
taken to task

stateless revolution
burns thru the night

wresting control
by any means necessary

no more unrest hidden
by the sleight of tyranny's tiny hands

the law for one
must be the law for all

and there will be no retreat
and no surrender
until then.

[a long year's night]

desolation streets
rolling thick with the smoke
and tears of standing ground

civility and protest pushed
to the final points of break

this wave will not subside
these fires will not cease to burn

until the rage
of generations unheard
is heeded once and for all.

[falling toward arrival]

even as the river fades

and our last goodbyes break
on the shore of forgetting

if we don't believe
there is something better
waiting for us

there never will be.

[equal vision]

my eyes have seen the burning
my heart has felt the weight

my silence will only betray the fight

the system is not broken
it was built this way

and anything short
of a complete tear down
will not bring the change needed
to remove the inherent injustice embedded
within the structure of a nation built
by the very hands, blood, souls, and strength
of those it continues to oppress.

[all rise]

humanity overrun
with black bodies broken and bloodied
by authority out of bounds

and though we may march in anger
we do so for peace

to protest is to survive
to remain silent is to condone the unacceptable

raise your voice
raise your fist

listen
learn

join the choir of change
speaking out in the name of justice and equality

and vow your truth, your promise,
and your unrelenting obligation
to power people forward.

[keeping peace]

simple requests
for great change

every channel
every street
every voice

together for a common purpose

that no more need to die
just trying to live.

[cease fire of the mind]

find the holy ground within
be it from sorrow, anger, or pain

allow a safe haven from the outside world
a space to rest, regroup, recalibrate

to cultivate a deeper strength

to breathe freely
so as to continue to fight
alongside those who cannot.

[the weight of things undone]

the circle widens
to break the blue line
and smash its shield

long this fight for growth and progress
for the killing and oppression of generation after generation of color
to become as common a fodder for revolution
as the white walled streets of privilege and pensions

nothing matters more than these lives lived in fear
now taking the power back and turning
burning page after burning page

until the smoke is cleared,
the pages are blank, and the
book can be completely re-written.

[codes and colors]

a none too hidden agenda
of militant intimidation

consistently reinforced
by authority's heavy white hand

have made inarguably necessary
the antidote now being administered;

if terror and supremacy
are built into the structure

the only way forward
is to tear it down.

[blind accomplice]

new light on old ideas
i see my part in past events

if only silence
and covered eyes
were the worst of it

but so much more
becoming prevalent
as i choose now
to listen and learn
instead of denying
any culpability or association

we all
must be held
accountable for our history
by acknowledging its mistakes
no matter how hidden or heinous

by choosing to ignore
these fatal errors moving forward,
we are blatantly disregarding our existential effects
upon the full spectrum of humanity.

[make way]

coming to ground
inside the city of your soul

screams turn silent
in the wake of rebellion

to care for the heart
as a respite to anger and injustice

to become centered and alone
with all within

is what will enable us
to consistently and vehemently

heed the calls to action that fuel
the unending revolution now underway.

[here is now]

waste not time
grappling with matters of fact
and those who deny them

these ugliest of truths
need to be acted upon
once uncovered

in order to disrupt the pipeline
of obfuscation and denial
callously constructed by those who
believe themselves to be above and beyond
any accountability for their soulless actions.

[this mourning]

eyes open
heart wide

sadness is only part
of the equation

let not the silence fester
and become regret

as the floodgates sway
on broken hinges

we are all the sparks
to a greater fire

disrupting to dismantle
breaking to rebuild
burning to reveal

the living, breathing proof
that the system is wrong

and together
we are the truth.

[keeping pace]

many set ways
remained unchanged
from previous generations

so much so
that reason and sense
got lost beneath the weight of tradition
and history

these molds are finally being broken

for no more can we rest upon
or accept the laurels
of what and how things have been
just because some people
fear it no longer being how it always has been

we have a say

we must never grow tired of change
change is truth

and truth is a persistent rebellion
against the ignorance of those
who refuse to evolve.

[all the way home]

fire traps the mind

as i try to unlock the bones of the brain
trapped in cacophony

pandemic and protest
isolation and injustice

solutions stalled by the blindness
and ineptitude of power and entitlement

progress denied by ancient rhetoric
and magical beliefs

make no mistake, it is time
that has chased our history down

a shameful parade of countless incidents

beating after beating
death after death
decade after decade

begging change with every occurrence

and now it has been cornered
giving time no other choice

but to demand an explanation
for every bloody lie
history has told.

[marks made]

fresh notches in this historic presence
nothing less than full acceptance and
an admission of every hidden truth

an advancing front
of forward motion
to tip the scales

this is the final shove every
previous push has provoked

and there will be no pause,
no appeasement, no truce,
no compromise, no surrender

until the demands are met;

this is the good hard rain
this starving, parched, and burning nation
has needed for far too long.

[no other day]

broken from the beginning
light spills thru the cracked darkness

the opening of eyes, hearts, sky

we are here again
to make what we will
to fight what we must
to live how we can

until the only shadows over our shoulders
are the children of a brighter dawn.

[plague of allegiance]

disruption is paramount
in rewiring system and structure
from the baseline of the soul's survival

within these instinctual cities of our being
as well as thru the scenic tributaries
of tactical advantage
outside our walls

change will chalk its initials
upon new monuments to humanity's
highest truth

while toppling the bygone monoliths
of lies and oppression
that only the most callous and clueless
of our collective species
continue to hold sacred.

[the breadth of change]

reconstruction in progress
with brighter visions present
from learning to listen

stronger weapons forged
within the fires of truth

holding forth in the falling night
the air breathes the words as the darkness ignites

something greater
than sums and parts

more powerful than the walls
history has erected

as thoughts like burning butterflies
emerge from beneath the shame of silence past.

[voyagers]

less reason than zero
to look back over our shoulder

there is nothing to be found in that direction
that has any hope of changing

much the same is the fantasy horizon ahead
we think we can reach without effort

the only chance we have to profoundly alter
the future in any positive way is to start right
this very second

destiny, fate, prophecy, and whatever other words
used to allude to happy endings of rapture and redemption
mean nothing unless our every step, every move,
every breath forward is a task to be undertaken
with the benefit of all beings in mind

a continuing harrowing and joyful journey
that can only have as much meaning as we give it
beyond our own myopic agenda of arbitrary necessity.

[right of way]

every dusk the sun falls
the night becomes our home

every dawn darkness lifts
its heavy curtain

to return to us the light
of which every midnight dreams

and we slowly awaken
often certain of nothing
but that we must rise.

[no coming, no going]

current spaces hard on the heart and mind
but where we need to stay to unfold these times

nothing else will lend the light we need to see
better than our own eyes

colored only by the most basic beliefs
that last beyond what we come to know
does not further our being

we must continue to push forward
with the weight of this very moment

letting go of all we thought
before we learned to know better.

[all at once]

our humanity is our salvation
and we are failing miserably

as one cohesive organism
we continue to degrade and regress

simple requests for solidarity,
kindness, and respect are literally
argued to death by some who believe
disharmony and denial are better answers

this repugnant disregard for the lives
and well-being of others stands in direct opposition
to the evolution and survival of a civilized society

and while i feel our doom is imminent
and far too close at hand because of this

i still hold the most precious and sacred hope
of being proven wrong.

[ride]

stowed within the waves
presence held in safekeep

rolling thru the crash and flow
matching the storm step by step

surfacing to breathe the light
and diving deeper to set fire
to the darkness below.

[a little something]

there is hope
on a saturday afternoon

haloed by the hard sun
behind the gray

a rose thru a dirty window
the lily in a house of death

yet for some
there is no light

and it is for those
i hope the most.

[backwards to nowhere]

hope falls further
as avoidable disarray
maintains no distance
among the herd

truth only heard
by its own choir

nothing to believe
but what you already think

progress thwarted again
by imbecilic entitlement to freedom
without responsibility.

[mind over matter over god over country]

hope is a slow burn
constantly counterpunched
by a severe lack of both understanding
and compassion

compounded by a disturbing trend
of anti-intellectualism that perpetuates
the denial and refusal to continue to evolve
or better learn the situations that surround us

even as we cross this increasingly pivotal threshold
from which to see everything anew and begin to heal
the wounds of history

there will still be those left behind
waving their long-defeated flags

unable or unwilling to come to terms
with their upbringing, their ignorance,
their pride, or their pain

and all that which must be done
to overcome it.

[everything leaves]

as much as we hold
nothing can stay

not the touch of autumn
on winter's breast

nor the ashes of the river
in the crook of your heart

as hard as we pray
or try not to

things will still hurt
as much as they hurt

no gods will meet us
to soften the blows

no dogs will bark our arrival
at the burning gates of nowhere

as we wander the catatonic buildings
of this world ensouled

nothing is inevitable
until after it happens

death is not a threat
but a promise

of the magnificent absence
of all this glitter and doom

and the greatest relief
of absolute nothingness.

[loneliness is a sunday morning]

sorrow like a shot
straight right thru

deep in the shallows
of wake and wave

pulled under by
the anchor of the heart

settled at the bottom
in darkened places unremembered

longing to be the light.

[there ought to be magnolias somewhere in this dusk]

screens and streets
alive with the sound
of revolution

as time
begins to break
from the weight
of history's pain

spilling out
a presence denied
for far too long.

[finding center]

a shame historic
brings profound weight
to these publicly personal proceedings

coming to light
within the context
of opposition and oppression

a new dawn of understanding
for many who assumed themselves
unaffected by and faultless of
the actions of our ancestors

thinking things had changed
thinking things were better now

and while that may be true
to some small extent

not nearly enough has been done
to level the playing field by those
who reap the benefits of its disproportionate advantage

so let us foster this change by locking step
with our brothers and sisters of all color

let us help further this equity of all beings
by deeply acknowledging the sins of our forefathers
and moving forward with newfound diligence and honesty

about what has been done, all that still needs to be done, what more needs to be learned, and how best to lend our hearts and voices to this fight above all else.

[mirror]

moving parts removed
an equation of one remains

an unsolved singularity

a reflection
of a shadow
in an empty room

lost
in a thought
of a dream of
a ghost

forever wishing
nothing was real.

[catching breath]

curtains pulled
keeping out the sun

the days hardly matter anymore
just numbers adding up
to a lonesome infinity

eyes closed
turned inside

standing on a cliff
overlooking the fields of the mind

flowers on fire with the love
of everything here and gone

as the heart smolders
somewhere in between.

[making space]

time removed from time
easing thru the abyss

mind away from mine
one returning to one

inward bound
the safe place of soul

to surround and become
what we have always been
again and again.

[as blood wakes on the ash]

lost
at the dying gates
of summer

winter's end
brought a springtime
of sickness

and our fall
seems continually
infinite.

[future considerations]

minus time
and its restraints

from a love riot mind
with a list of demands

nothing is ever in control

ghosts given up
for no expected reward

the necessary wounds of progress

scraping thru the briars of departure
as the cool calm of arrival awaits.

[souls to the wind]

swift as storm
fate is unsealed

we are but foundlings all
pitched forward into the sun of new life
at every turn

to put practice
into purpose

and bring lessons
to light

even through
our darkest times.

[live thru the heart]

be intimate
with life

with nature,
with culture

feel the soul
in all surroundings

see the gods
in all things

openly
and embracingly

to love
is to surrender

to the most
basic instinct
there is.

[unremoved]

out of sync today
not much clicking

soul sickness getting to me

stirred slowly crazy
by this staggered isolation
and continued tension

feeling an extra burden of responsibility
for those who seem to think they have none

need they be reminded
this is fucking crisis mode

and the weight is everyone's to bear

from pandemic to protest
our humanity is the sole link

between both our personal liberation
and societal transformation

and it's high time
we all start treating it as such.

god ~~bless~~ damn america

distance divided
access subtracted

self-preservation heightened
in light of scant evidence
of shared humanity

truth false-flagged
science scoffed at

let the aged die
so the young can beach go
and Karen can get a haircut

the least we can do
is extend further privilege
to all those unaffected by
brutality and discrimination

while others continue fighting
just to breathe…

during which time
the rest of the world
tightened up

heeded warnings
demonstrated grace
under severe pressure

while we fell apart
ungoverned and infighting

so this is where we are now
still sick, still suffering

unwelcome anywhere
beyond our polluted shores

sadly and
rightfully
so.

[becoming true]

seeing long stretches
of dark road
in both directions

as transformations resolve
discrepancy and alignment

and myths reveal deeper consciousness
from chasms thought uncrossable

we can only travel
at the speed of our own light.

[not everything that is real is true]

dictated by societal means
we are taught by our own existence

knowing not the impact
of our non-classification
in deeper schemes of acknowledgement
and bias

needing to broaden our spectrum
the more progressive we become

inclusivity is often overlooked
by those of us falsely believing
we are above such tensions and neglect

there are voices to guide us
and words to inspire us
outside of our wheelhouses

far beyond the scope
of what our own experience
has told us

we can only go so far
on what we already know

our specific status quo
needs to be unsettled,

our complicity challenged,
our comfort uprooted every so often

in order to constantly reevaluate
the truth of who we have been,
who we currently are,
and who we wish
to be.